The Moon

Written by
Paulette Bourgeois

Illustrated by
Bill Slavin

Kids Can Press

Acknowledgments

I am grateful for the help of the scientists at the McLaughlin Planetarium at the Royal Ontario Museum, and the Ontario Science Centre for sending information and answering questions. I am thankful that Terence Dickinson, a man who knows more about the skies than almost anyone else, made the time to read my manuscripts and make helpful suggestions. Bill Slavin was very patient and did a spectacular job making the science come alive. And finally, I would like to thank Elizabeth MacLeod, a wonderful writer and editor, who always asked the right questions and kept me on track.

First U.S. edition 1997

Edited by Elizabeth MacLeod
Text design by Marie Bartholomew
Page layout and cover design by Esperança Melo

Printed in Hong Kong by Wing King Tong Co. Ltd.

CMC 95 0 9 8 7 6 5 4 3
CMC PA 96 0 9 8 7 6 5 4 3 2

Published in Canada by   Published in the U.S. by
Kids Can Press Ltd.   Kids Can Press Ltd.
29 Birch Avenue   85 River Rock Drive, Suite 202
Toronto, ON M4V 1E2   Buffalo, NY 14207

Canadian Cataloguing in Publication Data

Bourgeois, Paulette
    The moon

(Starting with space)
Includes index.
ISBN 1-55074-157-8 (bound)
ISBN 1-55074-332-5 (pbk.)

1. Moon — Juvenile literature. 2. Moon — Experiments — Juvenile literature. I. Slavin, Bill. II. Title. III. Series.

QB582.B68 1995   j523.3   C95-930756-7

Photo credits
Bill Ivy: page 4, 28, 30. *K. Jackson, U.S. Air Force*: 27 (right). *NASA*: 8, 14, 16, 17, 18, 21, 28, 30, 32, 34 (both), 35, 36 (both). *G.E. Ulrich, Hawaii Volcano Observatory, U.S. Geological Survey*: 27 (left).

Contents

The Moon: Earth's nearest neighbor

**What looks bright but makes no light,
is a circle one day and nothing at all soon after,
looks as soft as cheese but is really hard as rock?
The Moon, of course!**

Moon tales

Long ago, people explained the riddles of the Moon with stories.

In Transylvania people believed the Sun was a king and the Moon was his brother. The Sun married a woman with golden hair and the Moon married a woman with silver hair. Their children were the stars.

The Sun thought the universe was too crowded so he decided to kill his children. But the Moon stopped him. That made the Sun so mad that he started chasing the Moon around the sky — and he's never stopped.

If you see a word you don't know, look it up in the glossary on page 39.

People in Papua New Guinea explained where the Moon came from with this story: There was only one old woman who knew the secret of fire. Whenever anyone needed fire she went into her hut and brought some out. One day some curious boys waited until the old woman left her hut. They sneaked inside and lifted the lid of a pot in the corner.

The Moon jumped out of the pot and leaped up onto the roof. As the boys followed, it jumped to the top of a coconut tree. One boy grabbed the Moon, but it was so slippery it slid away and flew higher and higher into the sky. It's still there and you can see the boy's fingerprints all over it.

What is the Moon?

The Moon is Earth's satellite and our closest neighbor in space. The Moon is a big rock with mountains, flatlands and craters (large, round holes).

The Moon is twice as big as the planet Pluto!

How does the Moon shine?

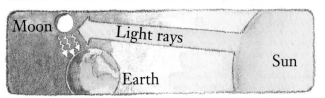

Moon | Light rays | Sun | Earth

The Moon shines with a lot of help from the Sun. The Sun is a star and makes its own light. The Moon makes no light. But sunlight bounces, or reflects, off the Moon. Without the Sun there would be no moonlight.

MOON FACTS

The Moon is about 390 000 km (240 000 miles) away from Earth. If you could walk to the Moon, it would take you almost ten years to get there.

The Moon is 3500 km (2200 miles) across, which makes it big enough to cover Australia.

The Moon weighs 81 million trillion t (tons). That's 81 with 18 zeros after it. Earth is 80 times heavier.

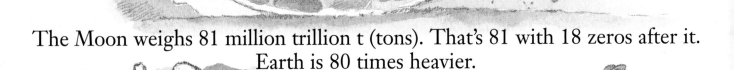

The Moon is over 4½ billion years old.

TRY IT!
Find out about the Moon's light

You'll need:
○ a bicycle reflector
○ a flashlight
○ a box or dark room

1. Look at the reflector in the dark room or put it in the box so that no light can reach it. Does the reflector shine?

2. Shine the flashlight on the reflector. Now does it shine?

The reflector shines because it reflects the light of your flashlight. The Moon shines because it reflects the light of the Sun.

Moon marvels

The Moon is a satellite of the Earth. A satellite is anything that circles around a planet. Some satellites are natural, such as the Moon. Others are launched into space by rockets. They beam information about space back to Earth or send TV or telephone signals.

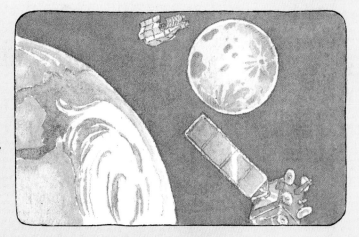

Is there life on the Moon?

Nothing can live on the Moon. There is no air for plants or animals to breathe. There is no water to drink. When the Moon faces the Sun it is too hot to grow anything. When it faces away from the Sun it is colder than the iciest place on Earth.

This is how the Earth looks from the Moon.

Is there wind or rain on the Moon?

No wind blows and no rain falls on the Moon because the Moon has no air or water. Wind is moving air and rain falls when there is water in the air.

We have air and water on Earth because of the strong pull of Earth's gravity. Gravity is the invisible force that holds everything on Earth.

When Earth was forming, gases escaped from its center. But Earth's gravity held these gases close to its surface. These gases became our air, or atmosphere.

The Moon's gravity wasn't strong enough to hold on to any gases that escaped from its core and they floated into space.

Where did the Moon come from?

No one is sure how the Moon formed. But scientists know that Earth and the Moon are about the same age and are made of the same types of rock. Maybe, long ago, when Earth was a hot ball of rock, a small planet hit it. Bubbling rock flew into space, then cooled and hardened to become our Moon.

Does the Moon move?

The Moon travels in a path called an orbit around the Earth. It takes almost one month — 27 days and 8 hours — to make one round trip.

You can only see one side of the Moon from Earth. It is called the near side of the Moon. The far side is always hidden from Earth.

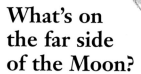

What's on the far side of the Moon?

The far side has many more mountains and craters than the near side, but not as many large seas. We knew nothing about the far side until 1959, when a spacecraft traveled around the Moon and took pictures.

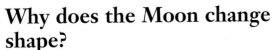

Why does the Moon change shape?

The Moon doesn't change shape. But as it moves around Earth you see only the parts of the Moon that are lit by the Sun. Sometimes you see only a small sliver of Moon lit up and sometimes you see the entire near side.

Each Moon shape you see is called a phase. The phases follow the same pattern every four weeks.

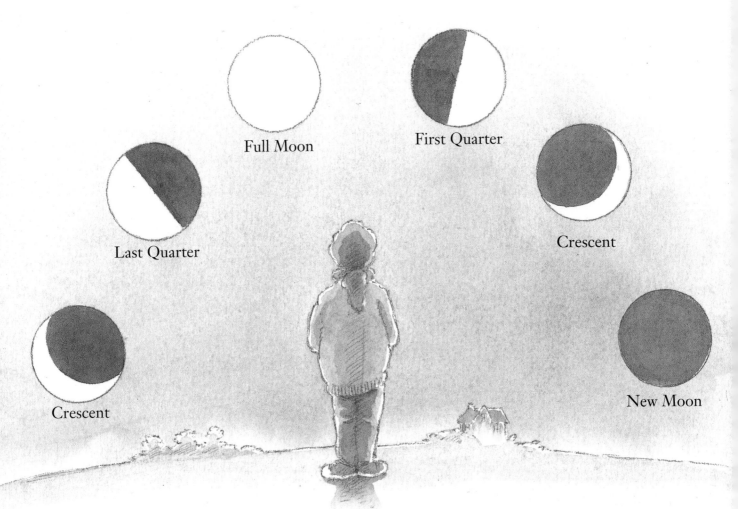

Full Moon

First Quarter

Last Quarter

Crescent

Crescent

New Moon

Why do the First Quarter and Last Quarter look like Half Moons?

The names really tell you how much of the Moon's monthly trip around the Earth it has made.

The first time you see a Half Moon it is called the First Quarter because the Moon has made one-quarter of its trip around Earth. Last Quarter means the Moon has only one-quarter of its trip left.

TRY IT!
Discover why the Moon has phases

You'll need:
○ a bright desk lamp
○ a dark room
○ a big, dark-colored ball
   such as a basketball

1. Pretend the light is the Sun, the ball is the Moon and you are Earth.

2. Stand a little way from the light with the ball in your hands. Hold out your hands so that your arms are straight and the ball is in front of you and a little higher than your eyes. You can see only the near side of the ball. No light shines on it. This is like looking at the New Moon.

3. Keep holding the ball out in front of you. Turn slowly in the same spot, away from the light. You'll see more light shine on the near side of the ball. When your back is to the light, most of the near side of the ball is lit up. This is like looking at the Full Moon.

4. Keep turning until you come back to your original position. Did you "see" a Crescent Moon and a Quarter Moon as you turned?

Since the Moon and Earth are always moving, the Sun does not always light the same parts of the Moon. You only see the parts that the sunlight hits.

When does the Moon rise?

The Moon rises at a different time and in a different place each day. The place and time the Moon rises changes because the Moon moves and so does the Earth. You can find out when the Moon rises by checking in a daily newspaper.

In northern countries, the Full Moon closest to September 22 is called the Harvest Moon. For a few days this Moon rises at almost the same time each night — right after the Sun goes down. It gives farmers lots of extra light to bring in their crops.

TRY IT!

Find out why a Full Moon looks bigger when it's low in the sky

You'll need:
○ a Full Moon
○ a dime

1. Look at the Moon as it is rising and is near the horizon.

2. Now turn your back to the Moon, bend over and look at the Moon upside down through your legs. Does it look the same size as in step 1?

3. Stretch out your arm and hold your dime up to the Moon. How big is the Moon compared to the coin?

4. Later in the night, when the Moon is higher in the sky, compare it to the dime again. Is it the same size as in step 3?

A Full Moon is always the same size, but your eyes play tricks on you. When you looked at the Moon upside down, you changed the way you saw the Moon and your eyes were no longer tricked. When you compared the Moon to the dime, you proved that the Moon is always the same size, no matter where it is in the sky. Scientists use experiments like this to learn how our eyes and brains judge size and distance.

A closer look at the Moon

Now we can take a closer look at the Moon
through binoculars and telescopes.
We can see its craters and mountains.
But in early times people did not know there
were any craters and mountains.
They only saw dark and light spots on the Moon.
So they made up stories to explain the mystery.

Man in the Moon stories

One Native American tale says a man and his dog are in the face of the Moon.

Another says there is a frog weaving a basket.

A German story says you can see a man with a broom and a woman with a butter churn. Other tales from Malaysia say there isn't a face in the Moon, just a hunchbacked woman fishing with a rat.

Here is a legend from Africa: Long ago the Moon did not shine and it was jealous of the Sun with its bright rays. So one day, when the Sun was on the other side of the Earth, the Moon stole some of its light. The Sun was so mad that it splashed the Moon with mud. You can still see those spots today!

The first person to take a closer look at the Moon through a telescope was the Italian scientist Galileo in 1609. He thought the large dark spots were seas. They're still called that today! Find out more about the Moon's seas on page 22.

Why are there light and dark spots on the Moon?

The dark spots are large, flat areas of dark rock. The light spots are mountainous areas made of lighter colored rock.

If you look at the Moon through a telescope you can see more dark spots caused by shadows of mountains on the Moon. With a telescope you can see other dark spots caused by the high sides of the Moon's craters blocking light from shining into the craters.

The astronauts on the *Apollo 11* spacecraft took this picture of a Full Moon. (For more about *Apollo 11*, see page 34.)

TRY IT!
Make Moon spots

You'll need:
- a dark room
- ten small building blocks
- a flashlight

1. In the dark room stand your blocks on a table, leaving spaces between them.

2. Stand back and shine your flashlight on the blocks from about 30 cm (12 inches) away. Look at the shadows the blocks make.

When you shine your flashlight on the blocks, you can see them clearly. That's because the blocks reflect the light. The mountains on the Moon do the same thing and when you look through a telescope at the Moon you see light spots.

On the far side of the blocks you can see shadows. On the Moon the mountains cast long shadows onto the flatlands. Those shadows are the dark spots you see when you look at the Moon through a telescope.

A big city would fit easily in this crater.

How are craters made?

Craters are deep pits on the surface of the Moon. You can see more than 30 000 Moon craters from Earth. The craters were made when space rock, called meteorites, hit the Moon. How does that make craters? Imagine throwing a big rock into a sandbox. When the rock lands, sand scatters up and out in a big circle.

That's what happens when a meteorite hits the Moon. Dust and rocks fly up and land in a big circle around the spot where the meteorite hit. That makes the high walls around the crater.

Many of the Moon's craters are named after famous scientists and astronomers, such as Galileo and others.

TRY IT!
Make Moon craters

This can be messy. Be sure you have an adult's permission before starting.

1. Pour a thick layer of dry plaster of paris into your bowl. Hold one of your rocks about 1 m (3 feet) above the container and let it drop. Do this with all the rocks but try holding them higher or lower above the bowl.

2. Carefully lift out the rocks and pebbles.

3. Gently spray your plaster with water until it is soaked. When it is dry, after about one hour, you can lift your model of the Moon's surface out of the bowl. Paint it gray to make it really look like the Moon, if you like.

The smallest and shallowest craters were probably made with small rocks you dropped from not very high above the bowl. The heavier the rock and the higher you held it when you dropped it, the bigger the crater.

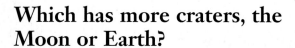

Which has more craters, the Moon or Earth?

The Moon has many more craters than Earth. This is not because the Moon is hit by more meteorites. It is because the rain and wind on Earth slowly erase the traces of craters on Earth. On the Moon, a crater stays the same forever.

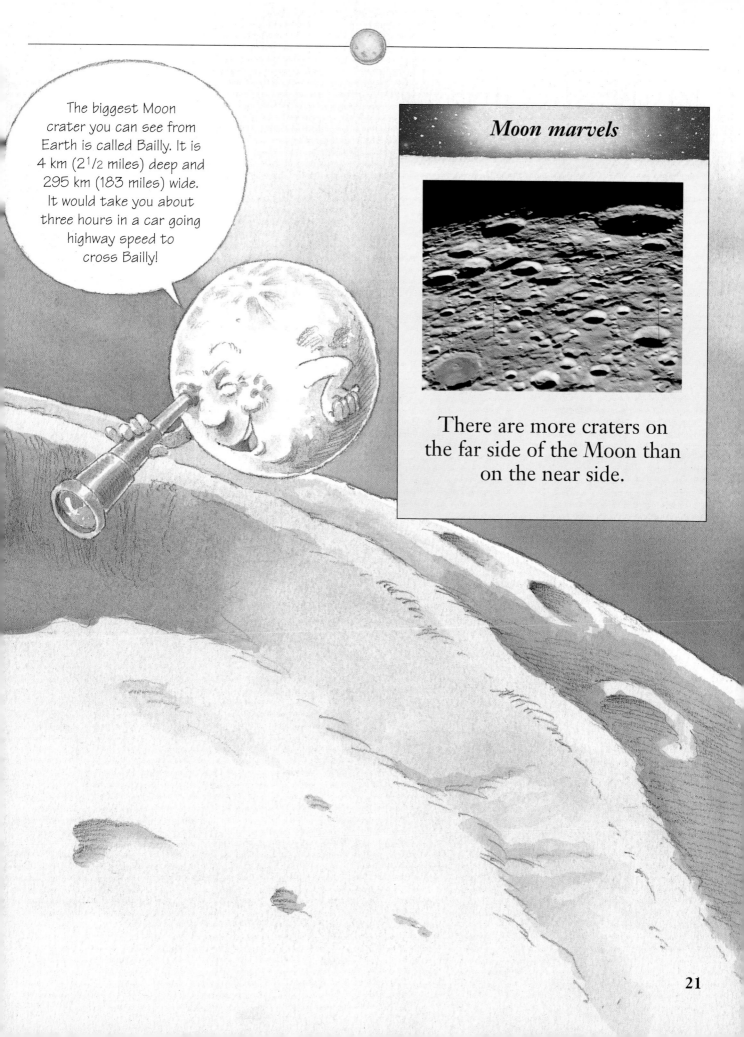

The biggest Moon crater you can see from Earth is called Bailly. It is 4 km (2$\frac{1}{2}$ miles) deep and 295 km (183 miles) wide. It would take you about three hours in a car going highway speed to cross Bailly!

Moon marvels

There are more craters on the far side of the Moon than on the near side.

What are the big, dark spots on the Moon?

Those big, dark spots are wide, flat areas of rock. Some people call them seas, even though there's no water in them. Scientists also call them maria.

Billions of years ago the Moon was hit by gigantic meteorites that melted vast areas of the Moon. When the melted rock (called lava) cooled, it became the maria.

All of the maria were given names by early astronomers. They have beautiful names, such as the Lake of Dreams and the Sea of Foam. The first astronaut on the Moon landed on the Sea of Tranquillity.

From Earth four of the seas together look like eyes, and a nose and mouth.
Look for them next time there's a Full Moon.

TRY IT!
Take a closer look at the Moon

You'll need:
- binoculars (get an adult's permission to use them)
- a dark night with a Full Moon
- a pencil
- a piece of paper

It takes practice to focus binoculars so you can see clearly with them. Ask an adult to help you.

1. Focus your binoculars on the Moon.

2. Draw what you see. Can you see mountains, seas and the round rims of the large craters?

You can see a lot more on the Moon when you use binoculars. Use the illustration here to help you fill in some of the details on your drawing. Sometimes when the sky is cloudy or full of pollution, you'll have trouble seeing the Moon clearly even with your binoculars. Try again the next night or when the next Full Moon is in the sky.

Moon watching

People have always watched the Moon because it
is beautiful.

People from long ago were also fascinated by the
way it changed from a Full Moon to a New
Moon and back. And they believed the Moon had
special powers.

Moon celebrations

Long ago, many people believed the Moon was a goddess who helped crops grow and brought women healthy babies.

In a special African feast of the New Moon, only women were allowed to celebrate. Just before the rainy season, they danced all night and prayed to the Moon to give them children and food for the coming year.

In tales from Hawaii, the Moon was called *Hina-hanaia-i-ka-malama*, which means "the woman who works in the Moon."

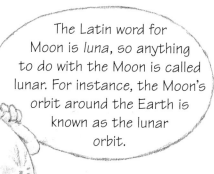

The Latin word for Moon is *luna*, so anything to do with the Moon is called lunar. For instance, the Moon's orbit around the Earth is known as the lunar orbit.

Chinese people all over the world celebrate the New Year on the day of the second New Moon after the shortest day of the year — that's sometime between January 20 and February 20. They believe that seven days before the New Year, the kitchen god goes to the heavens to report on the doings of the family. Chinese people offer him sticky molasses so he can't speak up and say anything bad about them!

During the festival of the Eighth Moon during harvest time, Chinese people hold a festival that includes dancing as well as parades with lit lanterns in different shapes. The most common lantern is a Moon shape, since it means perfect joy.

There are also many stories about strange things that happen under a Full Moon. Many people still believe that more crimes and weird things happen then. And there are lots of scary tales about people turning into wolves under the light of a Full Moon.

What is an eclipse of the Moon?

An eclipse of the Moon happens when the Sun, the Earth and the Moon line up in a straight line with the Earth in the middle. The Sun's light shining on Earth makes our planet cast a shadow on the Moon. We don't get a lunar eclipse every month because sometimes the Moon's orbit takes it a little above the Earth and sometimes a little below.

During a lunar eclipse, the Moon can be in the dark for over an hour. But it's never completely blacked out. Sometimes the way the sunlight is scattered and bent by Earth's air makes the Moon red.

A lunar eclipse once saved Christopher Columbus! The explorer and his men were in Jamaica and the native people didn't want to trade any more food with him. So Columbus warned them the Moon would turn red unless they helped him. He knew something the native people didn't — a lunar eclipse would happen that night. When the Moon turned red, the natives thought Columbus had special powers and gave him all the food he wanted.

Why does the Moon look blue sometimes?

The Moon can look blue when there is lots of dust or dirt in the air, such as after a volcano erupts or a forest burns.

The dust and ash act like filters and allow only the blue light in moonlight to shine through.

Every few years there are two Full Moons in one month. The second Full Moon is also called a Blue Moon, although no one knows why. But if you hear the saying "once in a Blue Moon," you know people mean something that doesn't happen often.

Moon marvels

Sunlight seems to be white or have no color but it is really a mixture of colored light. Moonlight is reflected sunlight, so it contains colors too. When moonlight hits a raindrop or dust, the colors fan out and you see some or all of the colors in a rainbow.

Can the Moon help you predict the weather?

When some people want to know the next day's weather, they don't turn on the radio, they look to the Moon. Many people believe that:

A Full Moon on Saturday means rain on Sunday.

Thunderstorms will happen two days after you see a New Moon.

A pale Moon means rain is coming.

A halo around the Moon means rain or snow.

Scientists don't believe most of these sayings but they agree a halo around the Moon often means rain or snow. The only time you see a halo is when there are lots of ice crystals high in the air. Lots of ice crystals mean clouds that will soon drop rain or, if it's cold, snow.

TRY IT!
Predict the weather with the Moon

You'll need:
- a pencil
- a notebook

You will need about five minutes each night for a month to do this project.

1. Watch the weather each day for a month. Report in your notebook if it was sunny or if it rained or snowed. Each night, look at the Moon and make a drawing of what you see. Write down the phase of the Moon (see page 10), whether the Moon is bright or pale and whether there is a ring.

2. When the month is over, look at your notes. Do you notice any patterns? If you saw a ring around the Moon, was there rain or snow the next day or the day after? Do any of the other sayings you just read about seem right?

You probably found that sometimes the sayings were right and sometimes they were wrong. Many things affect the weather and the Moon can't tell you about all of them. Take another look at your notes, then make up your own sayings about the Moon and the weather.

What are tides?

Tides are the rise and fall of water in large lakes, oceans and seas. At low tide, the water is pulled away from the beach, so there's lot of room for you to build sand castles.

But during high tide, the beach is covered with water.

Every day, on every ocean beach around the world, there are high tides and low tides. And they are caused by the Moon.

How does the Moon make tides?

As the Moon travels around Earth, the Moon's gravity pulls on the land and water on Earth. This pull changes the Earth's shape very slightly so that it bulges in two places. One bulge faces the Moon, the other bulge is on the opposite side of the Earth. Because water can flow easily over the Earth's surface, it gathers in these places and bulges even more than the land does.

As the Earth spins, the two bulges move to stay in line with the Moon, producing two high tides and two low tides every day.

TRY IT!
Follow the tides

You'll need:
○ an ocean beach
○ a notebook
○ a pencil

If you don't live near an ocean, you'll have to wait until you're on a visit there to try this experiment.

1. Look in the newspaper for the times when the high and low tides happen. Draw what you see at high tide. Can you tell by watching the water when high tide starts to come in or go out?

2. Draw what you see at low tide. What does the beach look like now?

There are two high tides and two low tides every 24 hours and 50 minutes. You can find the exact time by checking in a newspaper. The time between high tide and low tide is always the same.

On the Moon

Ancient people only dreamed about traveling to the Moon. But by 1959, scientists in the United States and in the former USSR (the Soviet Union) had already built the first space rockets. The race was on to see which country could be the first to land astronauts on the Moon.

Race to the Moon
(A real-life story)

First, both countries sent up spaceships without astronauts since they didn't know if people could survive space travel.

The American spaceship missed the Moon completely. A few years later, an empty Soviet ship made it to the Moon but it crash-landed!

The Americans sent seven more spacecraft into space. Only the last one sent back pictures of the Moon. The Soviets sent eight spacecraft, all named *Luna*, into space before they finally reached their goal. *Luna 9* landed softly on the Moon. Scientists knew so little about the Moon's surface that they were afraid the ship would sink into Moon dust, but it didn't. Now, they thought, anything was possible.

People around the world then wondered, which of the two countries would win the race to land astronauts on the Moon?

33

Who was the first person on the Moon?

It was an American who first stepped on the Moon. The American spacecraft, *Apollo 11*, took 66 hours to make the trip from Earth. The main spacecraft orbited the Moon while two astronauts flew down to the surface in a small landing craft. On Sunday, July 20, 1969, Neil Armstrong and Edwin "Buzz" Aldrin landed in the Sea of Tranquillity.

Neil Armstrong stepped out of the space capsule carrying a television camera. Everyone watching TV on Earth saw his first footstep onto the Moon. He said, "That's one small step for man, one giant leap for mankind."

Moon marvels

Because there is no wind or rain on the Moon, the footprints the astronauts left in the Moon dust will be there forever!

Astronaut Neil Armstrong took this picture of "Buzz" Aldrin. You can also see the landing craft they used to land on the Moon's surface.

What's it like on the Moon?

The sky is black and there are no colorful sunsets because you need an atmosphere to scatter the light to see the colors in it.

There is no noise because sound needs air to travel.

Earth looks like a giant blue ball.

The Moon's gravity is only one-sixth as much as Earth's. If you weigh 36 kg (80 pounds) on Earth, you'd weigh as little as a small dog on the Moon.

On the Moon, you could throw a ball much farther, jump much higher and feel as if you were doing a floating long-jump with every step! Every time you hit a baseball it would be out of the ballpark and out-of-sight!

You would be taller on the Moon. On Earth, gravity pushes the bones in your back tightly together. But on the Moon, the lower gravity means your back bones aren't packed so tightly. The extra space gives you extra height.

What did the astronauts do on the Moon?

Astronauts collected samples of Moon dust and rock to bring back to Earth so scientists here could study them to learn more about the way the Moon was formed. The astronauts brought back 382 kg (842 pounds) of Moon rock! They also explored the Moon's surface in "Moon buggies."

As well, the astronauts set up a device called a prism reflector. Scientists on Earth shine a laser beam at the Moon and this device reflects it back. The scientists know how quickly the light in the laser beam travels, so by measuring how long it takes for the light to return to Earth, they can tell more accurately than ever before how far the Moon is from Earth.

An astronaut scooping up Moon soil.

Moon marvels

Scientists had to invent many things for the astronauts — spacesuits, Moon buggies, space food and more. More than 500 of these inventions are now used on Earth, including pens that write upside down, video-game joysticks and Mylar, the material used to make bright metallic balloons.

TRY IT!

Make your own telescope

WARNING: IT IS NOT SAFE TO USE ANY TELESCOPE TO LOOK AT THE SUN.

You'll need:
- A mirror that curves inward, such as a shaving mirror or a make-up mirror
- a night when the Moon is shining
- a magnifying glass
- a small, flat mirror

1. Point the curved mirror toward the Moon.

2. Move your flat mirror as shown until you see the Moon's light in it.

3. Look in the mirror with your magnifying glass. The Moon should look closer and bigger.

In your telescope, the curved mirror does the same thing your eyes do — it gathers light so you see things. But a mirror can gather much more light than your eyes can. The Moon's light hits the curved mirror so that you see the Moon there. The flat mirror reflects the Moon to the magnifying glass. The magnifying glass makes the Moon seem bigger and closer.

This kind of telescope is called a reflecting telescope.

Will people ever live on the Moon?

Some day there will probably be a space station on the Moon. Many scientists would find it helpful. For example, astronomers could observe the universe from a Moon base. Since there is no atmosphere to cloud their view, they could see much more clearly from the Moon than from Earth.

The Moon station might also become a mining center for Earth. We are using up the metals and minerals here. But Moon rock is full of many of the minerals that we need and use.

Scientists might also make new medicines on the Moon. A germ-free place is needed for making drugs and since there is no life on the Moon, there are no germs there.

Of course, for people to live on the Moon they will need food to eat, air to breathe, water to drink, and gravity to help them move around comfortably. Right now we don't know how to do all these things, but in the future they may be possible. Perhaps you'll be the scientist who builds the first Moon base!

Glossary

astronaut: a person trained to travel in a spacecraft

astronomer: a scientist who studies stars, planets and other objects in space

atmosphere: the blanket of gases that surrounds the Earth

binoculars: an instrument that helps you see far-away objects more clearly

core: the innermost part of a planet, moon or star

crater: a round pit made by a meteorite, or by a volcano collapsing

gas: a form of matter made up of tiny particles that are not connected to each other and so can move freely in space. Air is made up of gases.

gravity: the invisible force that holds everything on Earth, keeps the Moon circling the Earth and holds the Earth and planets around the Sun

lunar: about the Moon

lunar eclipse: takes place when the Sun, Moon and Earth are in a direct line with the Earth in the middle. Earth casts a shadow on the Moon and the Moon seems to turn dark.

meteorite: a piece of space rock that crashes on the surface of a planet or moon

orbit: the path an object takes through space

phase: the different shapes of the Moon we see as the Moon circles Earth. The Full Moon is a phase of the Moon.

planet: a large object that circles a star and does not make its own light. Earth is a planet.

reflect: to bounce back light (Objects can also reflect heat and sound.)

rocket: an object that is driven into space by the explosions of burning fuel inside it

satellite: a small object that circles a larger body, such as the Moon circling the Earth, or a communications satellite circling the Earth

scientist: a person who studies science

spacecraft: a vehicle that can travel beyond Earth's atmosphere

spaceship: a spacecraft that is large enough to carry people

telescope: an instrument that makes very far-away objects seem larger and nearer. Telescopes are often used to look at planets and moons.

tide: the regular rise and fall of water in large lakes, oceans and seas. Tides are caused by the pull of the Moon on Earth.

universe: everything, including Earth, in space

Index